CW01647782

Value Your Character

" 10 character values to empower you and transform your life"

By Jennifer Umusu

Founder & CEO of The Character Well

In memory of Chief Michael Ogbe Umusu JP

ACKNOWLEDGEMENTS

This book would not have been completed without the help of all the 'crew members' who helped build The Character Well from a single idea (a raft) in 2009, to become a developed (a motor boat) non-profit organisation and the basis of this book.

I hope to include all those crew members who have been part of moving The Character Well forward:

My late husband, Michael for his useful criticism and corrections and his patience for giving me time and space to carry on.

My son William Umusu, First Director of The Character Well and designer of the first website, for his support and involvement from the very beginning.

Arron McCleaver, Formerly of Creekside Press, Greenwich, designer of The Character Well Logo which is now our official Trademark.

Ebenezer Oke, Graphic Artist - creator of our two pull up posters and first member of our Advisory Committee.

Michelle Howe, Journalist - For her Pro-bono work on the original newsletters.

Patrick Jesu, Pro-Bono Accountant from 2013 - 2019

Kenny Ogbor, first major donator – helped greatly with expenses.

Lily Olumese, Legal Advice/Research Volunteer from 2014 – 2017. Volunteer contact with Jubilee Centre, University of Birmingham.

Colin Morton, Creator of the present website and designer of background for all the study units.

Shirley Ling, Longest volunteer, long term support and review of various documents.

Donna West, Long term family friend and volunteer.

Jason Umusu, Promotional Leader 2024, Responsible for this book being available to the public.

Others who have contributed to the Character Well, read through book drafts and given useful advice including, Chew Yeen Lawes amd Nye Onosey amongst others.

Thank you all.

Table of Contents

POSITIVE VALUES – POSITIVE LIVES

Hello, my friend,

What made you open this book? Was it the word 'Values' or the word 'Character'? Did someone give you a copy? Whatever the case, I do hope you will gain some positive value from the contents.

This book is about the character values that lie hidden within each man, woman and child; and how by using a few specific character values each person can continue to develop themselves and pass positive information on to their loved ones.

What do we mean by Character Values?

A) CHARACTER:- The word 'character' has three different meanings:-

- A person in a novel, play or film
- A letter or mark in writing or printing.
- A combination of qualities that distinguish an individual person or group.

B) VALUE:- The word 'value' means something of worth, merit, importance, moral principle, and something to regard highly.

Therefore, character values are important moral principles that distinguish an individual or a group.

Character values are for everyone, from the various ethnic groups found in the bigger cities and towns; to children from the age when they start to understand the meaning of words, to our grandparents and pensioners meeting at Pop-in groups and especially for hard working parents who wish that they had more time to spend with their children; and everyone else who wants to enhance their own character and hence feel more positive about themselves.

The Character Well organization is one group that aims to encourage people to improve their own character values as an aid to self-development, and, also, as an aid to family and social cohesion. The organization's slogan is **'Value Your Character'.** We need to look inside ourselves, refresh and revitalize our own character values. If we do this our own lives and those of the people around us will be effectively changed in positive ways.

The Character Well organization promotes the following values:-

- Appreciation
- Caring
- Forgiveness
- Generosity
- Honesty
- Loyalty

- Patience
- Respect
- Responsibility
- Self-control

These ten values were chosen for simplicity of use and the fact that many other character values will slip into one of these ten headings. Any of these values can be studied individually, but it is a good idea to think about 'appreciation' as the first value, so that a positive attitude can be initiated from the start. Most people can find something about their life, or environment, that they can appreciate. One can, surely, appreciate and be grateful for eye- sight, which enables one to read and write, see the faces of people and see all the wonders and colours of nature.

Initial discussion on character values could encourage participants to list all known values under these ten headings; for example, 'gratefulness', 'thankfulness' and 'gratitude' come under the character value of 'appreciation'. However, everyone will have a different view of which character values are important to them, which values they want to improve, or discuss with family members and friends, so the various chapters of the Character Well values are designed for individual use in any order, or as a single subject. For example – the character value 'Respect' may be a subject that you wish to discuss within your family, or someone may want to think more about the character value of 'Forgiveness' for personal reasons.

How did we decide on these 10 character values as the ones for The Character Well? Initial research showed that other Character Value groups, particularly those in USA, have anything between five and fifty different values in their list, most reviewing one value a month. Within The Character Well group we wanted a smaller number of values that could be reviewed within a year, so within the organization we did our first audit. We gave friends and relatives a long list of character values and asked them to choose the values most important to themselves. Hence the final choice of the above character values.

Your own individual character values choices can be very big - as big as you want it to be; the aim of this book is to be a guide to help you reactivate, or improve, or increase your own character values. We then ask you to spread the information about character values to your nearest and dearest, including the children.

Involving Children and Young People

Society is changing as we all struggle for success and survival and the technological age is with us, growing so fast that some of us find it difficult to keep up with all the new devices and systems. Children often know more about technology than some adults! At the present time children are also very vocal. Gone are the days when children were seen but not heard.

Character values are important for children as well as adults. We do want children to have a voice – to put across their views, let us know of emotional and physical problems, discuss issues they are confused about and to take their proper places in society. Adults need to listen to their children, and in some cases, learn from them. Children and young people need to know how to effectively communicate with their parents and other adults. As parents we have an important role to fulfill, by communicating with our children and by example, being positive role models. Children also, need compliments for good behaviour, so that they can understand more about basic ethics, and know the importance of developing and improving their own character values. This will enable them to feel more confident to cope with life as they become independent adults.

Society is beginning to realise and discuss the importance of character values. There are several long-standing character value groups in the USA; 'British Values' has been the focus of the British government from 2014. The Jubilee Centre for Character and Virtues at the University of Birmingham has produced both a Primary and Secondary School curriculum based on character values. Their excellent research articles and resources are free to download. The Character Well, however, aims to work with other nonteaching groups, and individuals who would benefit from self-development by gaining more confidence in themselves and their ability to cope with life.

People and Society

Do you think the world has lost some of its values, discipline and dignity?

Every home, school, company and government needs 'rules' for its members, employers and employees to work together in an organised way as team members of that particular group, thereby achieving progress and fulfillment. This is where character values play an essential part in ensuring co-operation and unity within families and the wider community.

Every child, adult and elderly person is important.

Sometimes we do not realise how our life impacts on other people, 'like ships passing in the night' – but ships cause ripples, which get larger as the ripples travel outwards. We all produce 'ripples' in our lives; our actions and words can affect other people, near and far. Modern communication has made that 'ripple effect' much more obvious. We need to ensure that we send out positive ripples by our own example.

Some groups are having a very positive effect on other people's lives. Most charities and some of the big business groups use part of their profits for beneficial purposes, and they get recognized for these efforts; examples include Oxfam and the Red Cross charities.

However, because there is a lot of fear, anger, and even hate, in the world, mainly caused by greed and wars, trust in other people is fading away. A lot of people look for ulterior reasons why someone should want to help them. Of course, unfortunately, some people do have ulterior motives; but they must be people who do not know the positive impact of character values and how important it is to value their own character!

We need to change the elements of fear, anger and hate that exist in our society, and instead bring in caring, self-control and mutual understanding.

We may strive to become better people, but it is difficult sometimes to know right from wrong; even the difference between good and bad. There are so many groups of people with different views, beliefs, cultures and traditions, but there is always the universal 'golden rule' of ***'Do to others what you would have them do to you'.*** Respect for each other is one of the values discussed and you are all encouraged to review and improve on the character values you already have and pass on your values to other people by your own example.

Please join us on this exciting journey.

Reputation is what
others think of you.
Character is
who you are.

CHAPTER 1

Do you have a positive outlook, or are your thoughts all about what has gone wrong with your life? Should we not move forward and embrace life as it is? We cannot change the past but we can think about the present and possibly improve the future.

We believe that APPRECIATION should be our first character value as it helps us think about good things in our lives, therefore leading to a more positive outlook on life.

APPRECIATION

> "**Gratitude** is not only the greatest of virtues, but the parent of all others." ***Cicero 54 BC***

To appreciate something is to value it and to be thankful or grateful for it.

Appreciation is more than being grateful for good things or people in your personal life, it is also about appreciating the good things around you, or even things or people that you can't see! For example, we can all appreciate the world-wide work of charities such as 'Save the Children' and 'Water Aid'.

Here is a list of things in your daily life that you may consider worthy of appreciation:-

- People in your life; parents, siblings, helpful friends, teachers.
- Your house and home; A 'roof over your head' can be really appreciated when you think of all the growing refugee camps in war torn areas of the world and homeless people sleeping on the streets, even in your own country.
- Your health and your senses. Whatever your own health, there is always someone who has more health problems than yourself. Modern medicine is enabling a lot of people to live longer and so allowing them extended time with families and to accomplish their life plans. Your five senses, sight, sound, taste, touch and smell, enable you to function safely; each sense should be appreciated. In the Introduction of this book the important of sight was mentioned, but can you imagine the problems you could experience if you lost the sense of touch and could not know when you touch a hot pan, or burn yourself in some other way?
- Modern conveniences; e.g. Inside flush toilets; hot water, washing machines, freezers etc.! Anyone who has experienced power failure will have more appreciation for modern conveniences.
- Modern technology; what a boon to our current generation – Communications, IT, mobile phones; so many things available at the touch of a button!
- Happy events – a party, a holiday enjoyed, the changing seasons, nature's life cycles and life itself.

- We have so much choice of food to eat. A pause before eating in thankfulness for all the food available, is a way of appreciating what we may be about to eat, and to remember all those who are not so fortunate.

I am sure that we can all find someone or something to appreciate from this list.

Family, Friends & Colleagues

Most of you will have friends, family or colleagues. You spend time with them, discuss and work with them and you get to know their good and bad habits. Do you show those who are close to you that you appreciate their good qualities?

Not many people live a completely isolated life, but perhaps the few that do so, would appreciate our help more than others. Do you know the names of your neighbours? Do you check on them occasionally, especially if they are elderly, young parents, refugees or new to the area.

Families

Each culture will have different ways of showing appreciation to their family members and friends, but in all cultural groups a few words of congratulation or appreciation encourages a positive response. Even simple words of appreciation like 'Well done', 'Thank you' or 'I believe in you' have a beneficial effect on the recipient.

Friends and colleagues

It is important that you appreciate friends who you can rely on to listen and advise sensibly. Remember you are their friend too, and you need to listen to them as well.

You may also have friends at work. As colleagues, you need to work as a team to produce the best results for the company or organisation that you work for. Team work produces results, and with good results, all team members can appreciate each other.

Others

- Many charities and companies do excellent work helping various people in different need groups. Maybe one of your relatives or friends has had help or support from such a group that you can personally appreciate.
- Elderly people have more experience of life and can generally give younger people good advice which can generate mutual appreciation.
- Giving appreciation shows others that you are not taking them for granted and what they do is important to you.

Our Being

Have you ever thought about the wonderful way your body works - day in, day out? How everything fits together and works in union to keep you going? Any study of biology will show the wonderful inter-reaction of the body systems. Occasionally, things get out of order, illness occurs, but then we have qualified doctors, tests and modern medicine to appreciate.

One of the most amazing things to appreciate is that plants 'breathe' out into the air the oxygen that we need to live - and we breathe out carbon dioxide that plants use as part of their growing process! Our lives and the lives of all animals depend on plant life.

Therefore, you need to care for your own body but also think about and appreciate your environment. The environment is essential for your own life and wellbeing.

Appreciate the beauty all around you

Open your eyes - look around you. There are so many things to appreciate.

- Marvel on the wonder of sun, rain and wind, and the importance of each in the cycle of nature.
- See the power of birds in flight - many birds fly thousands of miles when they migrate each year, and yet they can fill the morning air with their sweet musical calls.
- Appreciate the changing seasons - Spring, Summer, Autumn, Winter - each has its own period of beauty.
- And flowers - well – what a choice of colours and scents all year round from snowdrops to mistletoe and all the exotic plants that are now available from other countries.
- Look down - at the earth under your feet. Grass growing, and an earth teaming with insect life, all part of life's cycle of pollination and rebirth. Even in the ground itself the humble earth worm is busy tilling the earth for us!

Maybe you live in a town or city, a visit to a nearby park can help you think of the beauty all around you that can be appreciated.

Nature's Puzzle

Do you realise that everything in nature fits together like pieces of a jigsaw puzzle? If one piece is missing the puzzle picture is not complete. So it is with nature, and we need to ensure that none of the pieces go missing!

What does this mean?

Well, we need rain and sun to make crops, grass and trees grow. Crops give us basic foods like rice, cereals and bread. Animals eat grass, and from them we get food and clothing. Trees provide wood for housing, furniture and paper - so we need to renew the things we use, or there will be missing puzzle pieces! This is where an interest in recycling and care of the environment is so important

Do you appreciate our wonderful world? The world supplies all our needs, and we need to care for it in return. So please be more aware how you use Nature's bounty, don't waste it - replant, replace or recycle what items you can, and we will all find more appreciation for our world.

Modern Communication

We are long past the early days of communication - smoke or flag signals, pony express and telegrams! Communication systems are progressing so fast it is difficult to keep up to date with all the new technology. We can, however, certainly appreciate communication systems that allow us to speak to our family members thousands of miles away.

The Internet is a modern wonder, allowing us to study, research and learn about so many different things at the touch of a button. We can, and should, appreciate and make use of this modern technology to improve our knowledge, our lives and the lives of our fellow human beings.

We all rely on modern communications these days but we do need to realise that machines cannot replace direct human contact and communications that enable us to appreciate each other more. Families need to teach their children more about appropriate place and time and safety rules for answering text messages and e-mails, and the importance of verbal contact.

Summary

This chapter is meant to help you think about things in your life that you can appreciate regardless of your own circumstances. It shows just a few of the things that you can appreciate and give thanks for. If you feel in a 'down' mood, thinking of things in your life that you appreciate can make you feel more positive. Perhaps at the end of each day you could take a few minutes to think about the good things that have happened during the day, and what you are thankful for, thereby going to sleep with positive thoughts. Also, make a point of telling other people about something you appreciate or are thankful for - give a positive buzz to your life and the lives of those around you.

It is interesting to note that there is research into the benefits of being thankful and the benefits include greater happiness, better health, less depression, more productive life style. Therefore, it is obvious that appreciating the good things in your life leads to a more positive outlook on life as well as improved health.

A simple activity for you:-

What three items in your life do you most appreciate?

Appreciation Quotes

"By appreciation we make excellence in others our own property."

Voltaire – A great French Philosopher and writer. 1694-1778.

"There is more hunger for love and appreciation in this world than for bread."

Mother Teresa of Calcutta – 1910-1977. Albanian-born Indian Missionary.

Nobel Peace Prize in 1979.

"The way to develop the best that is in a man is by appreciation and encouragement."

Dalia Lama – Head of the Dge-lugs-pa order of Tibetan Buddhists. Born 1935

Nobel Peace Prize in 1989.

HONESTY

Honesty and integrity are absolutely essential for success in life – all areas of life.

The really good news is that anyone can develop both honesty and integrity."

ZIG ZIGLAR

CHAPTER 2

So where do you go from here?

Which of your character values
would you like to improve?

Do you want to follow a list or choose
one special character value?

The choice is yours.

We also are choosing a different order from the original alphabetical list. Why? Well, a kind friend recommended that before anyone can improve their own character values, they need to be honest with themselves about their own faults and needs. Hence our next character value to think about is Honesty!

HONESTY

What does honesty mean to you?

To us honesty means telling the truth. It means being truthful in what you do as well as what you say. Honesty is all about being sincere, truthful, honourable, trustworthy and genuine.

We believe that with honesty there is less chance of misunderstandings, confusion or conflict; and being honest protects innocent people from being blamed or punished. Also, other people may trust you more when they know that you are an honest person.

"If you tell the truth you don't have to remember anything."

Mark Twain 1835– 1910 American Author & Humourist

Honesty with Yourself

Most of us talk about other people, their good and bad traits, without thinking of our own good and bad traits! It is very important to 'look at yourself', understand how you tick:-

- What are your good points?
- What do you find difficult to deal with?
- What are your bad attitudes or habits?
- Do you ever cheat?
- How do other people view you?
- Do you worry about what other people might say about you?

Consider making lists under the above headings. If you are truly honest with yourself, you will be surprised at the results.

If you are honest with yourself about your character values, and try to make use of your good values while aiming to improve your poor attitude or habits, then you will gain increasing confidence and self-respect. One great advantage of self-respect is that you find that you do not mind what other people think or say about you, because YOU know that you are doing the best you can with your life and circumstances.

One example of honesty can be taken from Mark King, who won the Northern Ireland Open Snooker competition in November 2016. In his victory speech, Mark acknowledged the support of his family and spoke about the gambling problems he had in the past, and that he still attends GA meetings. By speaking about this openly Mark not only shows he has learnt to cope with a huge personal problem, but is an honest example to others with similar problems.

"You will never find yourself until you face the truth."

Pearl Bailey 1918 -1990, American Entertainer.

"The first thing is to be honest with yourself. You can never have an impact on society if you have not changed yourself. Great peacemakers are all people of integrity, of honesty, but humility."

Nelson Mandela, 1918 - 2013, Nobel Prize for Peace 1993, Anti-apartheid revolutionary politician, Peace Activist, President of South Africa 1994-1999.

Honesty with Others

Once you have been truthful about yourself you find that you can see other people in a different light, know more suitable ways to discuss issues with them, and generally achieve better outcomes for anything that needs discussion.

For myself, I have been on the receiving end of honest advice to good effect. I gave the original manuscript of this book to a few friends to read, one friend came back with the honest comment that she found it boring! She gave me advice on the content and layout which made me revise the whole book. I hope you will approve the final outcome.

We often say that 'honesty is the best policy' but rather than just a policy, honesty is an important character value. Policies change but values rarely do. When you are an honest person progress can be made and friendships cemented, and other people know that they can rely on you. Also of course, if you tell the truth, then you don't have to worry about trying to remember what you said previously and to whom!

Of course, in cases when it would hurt others to be completely honest, as when you want to encourage others to do better, you can temper the truth with alternative positive statements, while showing respect and a desire to help. It is important to remember that how you say something is as important as what you actually say.

Being untruthful is rather like a snowball that gets bigger and bigger as it rolls along and gets more and more difficult to stop. Lying requires a lot of effort and can cause stress and anxiety and if people believe a person is telling lies, they may not believe that person when they actually do tell the truth!

Truth and Trust

Whether you are at home, in the country, in the city or at work it is important to be able to trust other people close to you. If there is trust between people or within the family environment, everyone works as part of a team and great results can be achieved.

Trust cannot be achieved without truth. Truth means that you are correctly representing the facts under discussion.

Within the family unit honesty is vital so that children feel able to trust their parents for good honest advice, and therefore are able to discuss truthfully with their parents any information or problems relevant to their care; or even concerns they may have about their friends.

If you are a manager of a company or an organiser of a group then honesty amongst employees or members is important so that plans can be adjusted to achieve the best possible outcomes.

Trust and Confidence

Having confidence in being honest with each other leads to long term relationships

Trust and confidence go hand in hand, and both rely on honesty.

In other words:- Honesty + Trust = Confidence

This fact is relevant whether it involves a partnership in business, marriage or simple friendship. Within larger establishments such as businesses, manufacturing units, health units and the armed forces, it is vital to have that confidence in each other so that a team spirit is maintained and the objectives of the business or operation are achieved.

A confident person knows their own limitations, but is able and willing to pass on their knowledge to others. Being part of a confident team or partnership can give one a feeling of fulfillment, satisfaction and even happiness.

"Confidence...thrives on honesty, on honour, on the sacredness of obligations, on faithful protection and on unselfish performance. Without them it cannot live." Franklin D. Roosevelt; 1882 – 1945; 32nd USA President 1933-1945

Gossip!

Gossip is:- 'The oldest and most common means of sharing facts and views but also has a reputation for the introduction of errors and variations to the information transmitted.' *Wikipedia – the on-line encyclopedia*

Gossip is :-

- A group of people talking about someone else who is not present
- Usually hearsay, hardly ever from original source.
- Easily extended or misunderstood.
- Gossip is often negative.
- Can be a real problem, a cause of friction between different people.

Gossip is the idle talk or rumours especially about the personal or private affairs of others.

- Although it may start off with true facts as the gossip is spread so the truth gets distorted or exaggerated.
- Other people present give their own views on the matter, hence the information often ends up embellished with other details that may or not be true, and the original facts can get very distorted, so causing unnecessary friction between different people, and often leading to quarrels.

When you are honest about yourself you soon realise that gossip is best to avoid, often negative and misleading. Find positive issues to discuss and point out a person's good points instead of gossiping. This benefits everyone involved.

The Bottom Line

Honesty **is** the best policy, and an important character value. Why?

Truth will come out - someday, somewhere the truth gets known, and then there can be long term issues and problems to sort out if you were the one not being honest. However, if you always have a clear mind and are honest you can work and liaise with friends, relatives and colleagues without worrying about what you said and to whom.

Honesty displays character and builds a level of trust that is difficult to earn. Other people will also know you as a sincere, trust-worthy person, and that gives you a good reputation.

Also, as you work with more character values you will find that many of them are linked together. For example, once you are honest with yourself then you gain more respect for yourself and consequently learn to take more responsibility for your action, and by doing that find that you have more self-control over your life. Hence leading to your own self-development! It sounds easy when put like that, doesn't it, but if you value your character great things can be achieved.

Honesty Quotations

"Whoever is careless with the truth in small matters cannot be trusted with important matters" Albert Einstein; 1879-1955; German - born Physicist

"Honesty is the first chapter in the book of wisdom"

Thomas Jefferson; 1801-1809; 3rd USA President

RESPONSIBILITY:

"Concern yourself more with accepting responsibility than assigning blame. Let the possibilities inspire you more than the obstacles discourage you."

RALPH MARSTON

CHAPTER 3

Are you responsible for the care of another person?
Can you take responsibility for your own actions?
Do you think responsibility is an important character value?

RESPONSIBILITY

What does the word 'Responsibility' mean?

According to Webster's New World Dictionary 'responsibility' is:-

A condition, quality, fact or instant of being responsible; obligation, dependability etc.

And - **A thing or person one is responsible for.**

Responsibility can, in fact, be applied to different circumstances and therefore come under different headings e.g.:-

- Moral responsibility
- Social responsibility
- Family responsibility
- Legal responsibility
- Media responsibility

Therefore you can see the word 'responsibility' has wide implications and as a character value has an important part to play in your life.

Are you prepared to take responsibility for the actions that you take in your life, which may fall into one or more of the above groups? Will you teach your children responsibility? **We do hope so**.

Responsibility to Yourself

How much responsibility do you take for yourself and your actions?

- Do you take responsibility for your own actions? This leads to self-respect.
- Do you care for yourself, so that you can deal effectively with the important issues and people in your life?
- Do you realise responsibility is a stepping stone between the character values of 'patience' and 'self-control'? If you have patience, you are more likely to take responsibility for your own actions and with the character value of responsibility you have more self-control over your life.

Most of us lead hectic lives, with financial and emotional pressures. Juggling responsibilities can be difficult, especially if you have a demanding job and a family to care for as well.

We suggest that:-

- You need enough sleep, eight hours a night is recommended. Tiredness can play a part in how you react to problems.
- You take some recreational time to refresh yourself mentally and physically. It could be a hobby, therapy, a holiday, a family outing or just 'chilling out' to music.

- We suggest you make daily and monthly plans to include this 'me time'. It will improve your lifestyle and attitude in a positive way.
- Another responsible way to care for yourself is to be aware of when 'things are getting too much for you'. We all have these times, and the important thing is then to off-load some jobs or responsibilities to others. Within a family setting that is 'sharing responsibilities' such as housework; or at work it may mean 'delegating' some jobs to other members of staff. Giving responsibilities to others will make them to feel more positive about themselves and encourage them to work with you as part of a team effort, whether at home or work.

Responsibility Within Your Family

Does your family work as a team?

Every member of a family should have their own responsibility, and parents have a responsibility to teach their children that fact. For example, children could be given the responsibility to care for their own room and clothes. To survive and thrive as a family there needs to be team work, each member of the family with certain responsibilities to ensure smooth running of the household and peace amongst its members.

Mutual love and respect, of course, play a big part in happy family life and parents have a major role in ensuring the stability of the family unit. Think about having some quality 'family only' time at least once a month, either as a family outing or a sit down session to discuss family issues. Try to ensure that your children feel able to discuss their views with you at any time. Responsibility within the family unit is very important.

Responsibility at Work

Are you employed or do you work for yourself?

Does employment plays a major part in your life?. Work is a means of financial stability, but it takes a great deal of personal time. If you enjoy, or gain personal satisfaction from your employment, then you are blessed.

Whatever your job, teamwork is essential, each person having their own role and responsibilities to ensure that the aims or end products of the company or group that you work for are achieved. Rather like a family setup, each employer and employee has their own place and responsibilities within the chain of command to ensure maximum results for the organisation. If everyone takes their responsibilities seriously real results and satisfaction are achieved. So, if you are an employee, in whatever capacity, you need to responsibly ensure that your part in the project is successfully achieved.

You need to be aware of the aims and objectives as well as the Health and Safety regulations of the company that employs you. Having a good management team is necessary for overall achievement, as no company or organization can succeed without everyone pulling their weight, and that is an individual act of responsibility i.e. taking responsibility for your own special role within the team. **BE PART OF THE TEAM**

If you work for yourself then you have a responsibility to keep to deadlines and the quality of your work, so that your clients are satisfied with your work / product.

Responsibility to Society

We do have a lot of responsibility in our lives; to care for ourselves, our children and our families. If you belong to a big family it is sometimes difficult to even keep in touch, or to care for them all. But you do also have a responsibility to your local society and the country where you live to ensure a peaceful and progressive society. In most cases your local environment is very diverse, people of different cultures living in the same area.

It is therefore, important for you to ensure that the right people are responsible for organizing your local or national government, to ensure adequate facilities and suitable laws to maintain stability and peace. As responsible citizens, you should take up your right to vote for those in government, after carefully reviewing the different party manifestos and their chosen leaders.

On a more personal level, could you represent your local area? Maybe become a member of a school board, a director or trustee of a local charity or even a local councilor?

TAKE PART—HAVE YOUR SAY

Our Environment

Do you take some responsibility for your local environment?

There is much talk these days about global warming and the effect it is having on the changing weather pattern and our environment. Are you taking enough personal responsibility for this global change? Or are you putting the blame on governments?

We all have a part to play in this scenario, where even little actions will help protect our environment and the beauty of the world for our children's children. You can show responsibility by caring for the immediate environment you live in, and taking an interest in what is happening globally.

How can you do this?

1. Recycling is the first thing that comes to mind, with the safe disposal of non-recyclable items. Most local councils now have recycling systems; and schools are making children more aware of environmental issues. Be careful how you dispose of plastic bags and waste food.
2. You can 'car share', or take the bus, this helps to cut down on carbon emissions. Walking is good for your health as well as the environment. It is also good to see that cycling is becoming more popular as a means of travelling.
3. Be responsible, share the message about caring for your environment.

HELP SAVE OUR WORLD

The Bottom Line

Most of us are responsible for our own actions, whether we own up to it or not. There are very few people who act 'blindly' without thinking of the consequences to themselves or others; and a large percentage of those 'blind' actions occur in emergency situations.

Whether you are prepared to take responsibility for your own actions is another matter.

What happens in your life does affect other people—'the ripple effect' - and those ripples can be of a positive or negative nature.

To improve society you need to ensure that the ripples you send out are of a positive nature, so enabling others to feel good about themselves, improve their own lives and pass the ripples onto others.

It is not a difficult thing to do—a smile, a compliment, a hug, even an apology, or admitting when one is wrong shows others that you are sending positive ripples to other people and taking responsibility for your own actions.

Improve your character value of responsibility and see the positive effect it has on your life and the life of others close to you.

Responsibility Quotes

"Until the great mass of the people shall be filled with the sense of responsibility for each other's welfare, social justice can never be attained."

Helen Keller, 1880-1968; American Author and Educator who was blind and deaf.

"Character isn't something you were born with and can't change, like your fingerprints. It's something you weren't born with and must take the responsibility for forming."

Jim Rohn, American Author and Motivational Speaker.

"Responsibilities gravitate to the person who can shoulder them."

Tom Stoppard, b 1937; British Playwright.

RESPECT

When you are content to
simply be yourself And
don't compare or compete,
Everybody will respect you."

LAO TZU

CHAPTER 4

What do you understand by the word respect?
Is it different from idolizing, or veneration?
It certainly is not fear or awe. How can
one explain the word 'respect'?

RESPECT

Collin's English Dictionary gives the meaning of respect as 'deference or esteem'

Respect means showing regard and appreciation for the worth of someone or something, this includes:-

1. Respect for yourself.
2. Respect for the rights and dignity of other people.
3. Respect for people who live positive life-styles to help others.
4. Respect for the importance of your environment.
5. We also need respect to collaborate with other nations towards a peaceful world.

"Without feelings of respect, what is there to distinguish men from beasts?"

Confucius; 551-479BC; Chinese Philosopher, politician and educator.

Quote taken from ThinkExist.com

Respect Yourself

Can you respect other people if you do not have respect for yourself?

- With self-respect you feel confident.
- You appreciate what you have.
- You care about other people, understand different points of view.
- You have a sense of responsibility for your own actions.
- With self-respect you know that you are doing the best you can with what you have.
- Self-respect is a good feeling.

The way that you behave affects the way that people think of you. When you have self-respect other people are aware of your confident nature, know that you respect their views and that they can rely on you and therefore other people will respect you.

We need to understand that respect is different from pride. Pride can be a tendency to conceit - a tendency to think of one's own self-importance. Pride can lead to vanity and vanity does not go with self-respect.

So how do you gain more self-respect? Our character values of honesty and responsibility can give some guidance. We are all different with different problems affecting our lives, but if you value your character and work towards improving your character you will definitely gain some self-respect.

"There is overwhelming evidence that the higher the level of self-esteem, the more likely one will be to treat others with respect, kindness and generosity."

Nathaniel Branden; b. 1930 ; Canadian psychotherapist.

Quote from ThinkExist.com

Respect for Others

You show respect for others when you treat them the way that you like to be treated ourself.

" *- For to be free is not merely to cast off one's chains, but to live in a way that respects and enhances the freedom of others."*

Nelson Mendela; b 1918; South African Statesman; Nobel Prize for Peace 1993

Quote from ThinkExist.com

The above quote seems to sum up what needs to be said in this section about respect for others, but this is relevant to peace as well as freedom. This includes peace amongst family, friends and colleagues, as well as between nations and governments.

These are big issues from one little word—RESPECT.

How can you help this to be achieved?

- Listen and learn about others.
- Accept that others are different from yourself.
- Respect other people's views, while also explaining your own views.
- Be genuine in your attitudes.
- Encourage dialogue.

- Share knowledge.
- Give truthful advice.
- Appreciate other's input or help.
- Keep to agreements.

These points are relevant to ensure respect for yourself, your family and any group or society.

Emotional Environment – Raising Self-Esteem

The environment in which you grow up plays a large part in your attitude and respect for everything in and around your life. That is one reason why family values of love and respect are so important. Teaching children from a young age to respect other people and care for their toys etc., can have a lasting effect.

We do realise, however, that even with a good early life, one can make mistakes or wrong choices later in life, or events may occur that can affect how you feel about yourself and how other people respect you. It then becomes a question of attitude. Can you rise above the situation and make small changes to improve your self-esteem? By the very act of trying to change negative things in your life you will gain self-respect, and find that you are behaving more positively. This has a ripple effect; people close to you notice the positive change in your attitude and respond in a like manner.

A positive attitude improves self – esteem and aids mutual respect

Respect for Nature

You are part of the chain of nature. You need the sun and rain to grow your food, and provide vegetation for food and shelter for many animals. None of us can live without water. However you look at it we are all part of nature, and as such you should respect your own body, and take care of yourself as best as you can.

You do also, need to think of nature close to you, and how you can care for the environment in which you live, for example, by clearing away rubbish and providing flowers and habitat for small animal life to flourish. The ever-present plastic bags and bottles are an example of items that needs to be disposed of correctly. Plastic items lying around on the ground, in ponds and trees adversely affect the environment.

The power of nature is phenomenal; sun, water, wind and fire are all essential parts of life providing food, heat and energy. These elements are so powerful that they can also be destructive e.g. floods, forest fires, cyclones etc. Nature needs to be kept in a balance to function to its full potential. What is removed should be replaced or recycled.

Do you respect nature? For example - avoid wasting food & ensuring that items, like glass and tins are recycled correctly. YES...... NO...... UNSURE.......

Respect for Authority

Children and adults need to respect authority for harmony to be maintained in society.

For children, this means respecting your parents and teachers and other people who teach and advise you how to cope with life, besides guiding you through your education.

For adults this means having respect for the laws of your community and your country; in other words - to be law abiding citizens.

Respect should be a fundamental right for all human beings, but is not possible where there is prejudice and hate. Relationships and contacts that are built without respect are unlikely to be sustainable for long periods. If there is no respect for authority societies can break down. This is why those in authority also need to have respect for those they care for, and listen to their complaints and suggestions.

True respect is the first positive step to building relationships. Respect is also important in conflict situations, whether within the family, at work, within a group or even at a national level. This is because if respect is present people will listen to each other's points of view and discuss more openly, rather than reverting to arguments.

The presence of respect can create opportunities for positive dialogue and discussions towards peace in any group or society.

Do you encourage respect? For example - within your family or amongst colleagues.

The Bottom Line

Perhaps the best item to end with is a quote

from Mark Twain ; 1835- 1910 ; American author & humourist

"Ah, well, I am a great and sublime fool. But then I am God's fool, and all his work must be contemplated with respect.

Quote taken from ThinkExist.com

Definitely Mark Twain had a sense of humour, but this reminds us of our own imperfections, the wonders of creation, including ourselves, and the need to respect ourselves and each other.

In this age of social diversity and worldwide communication respect has a major role to play in solving some of today's difficult issues. To respect others one needs to understand their point of view, communicate and learn from each other. In simpler words - to know the good from the bad, respect the good in others and share beneficial ideas for the progress of the whole of humanity.

Make a list of people that you respect, in your family, at school or college and those you work with. People you respect are ones who can help you progress and steer you on the right road to a fulfilling life.

Respect Quotations

"Relationships flourish when individuality, freedom and growth are respected." Master Jin Kwon, b 1957; South Korean Martial Arts master.

"Respect yourself if you would have others respect you." Baltasar Gracia, 1601-1658; Spanish Philosopher and Writer

"Show respect to all people but grovel to none." Tecumseh, 1768-1813, Native American leader of the Shawnee and a large tribal confederacy that fought to retain Indian lands.

"You should respect each other and refrain from disputes; you should not, like water and oil, repel each other, but should, like milk and water, mingle together." Gautama Siddhartha, the founder of Buddhism 563-483 B.C.

"Among individuals, as among nations, peace is the respect of other's rights." Benito Juarez, 1806-1872; Mexican President (1861-72)

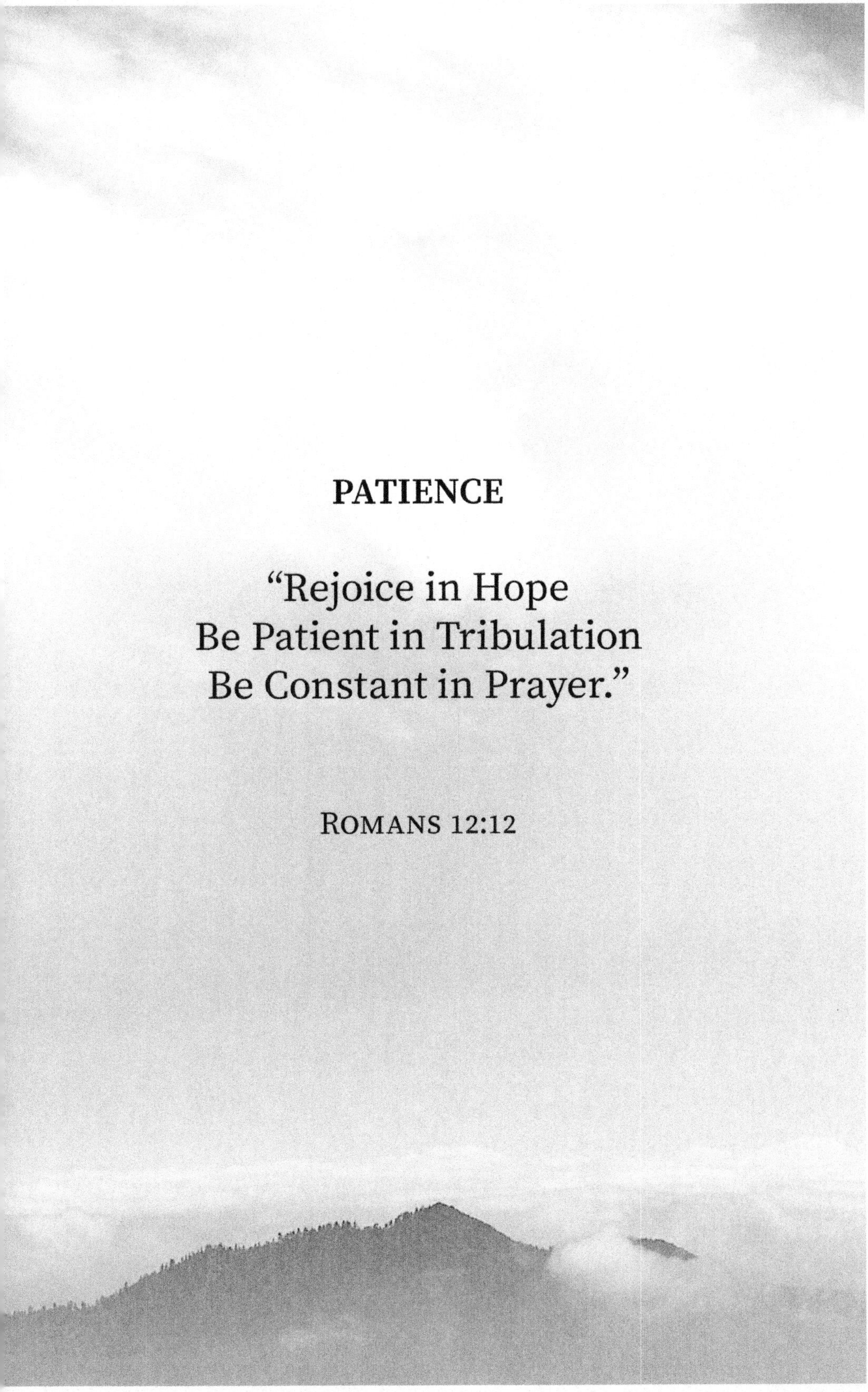

PATIENCE

"Rejoice in Hope
Be Patient in Tribulation
Be Constant in Prayer."

ROMANS 12:12

CHAPTER 5

PATIENCE

Definition of patience - noun - the capacity to endure or wait patiently.

There is an old rhyme about patience—

'Patience is a virtue,

rarely ever seen,

seldom in a woman,

never in a man'.

Now that is a good discussion point.

Is it true?

Patience with Yourself

You will find that the character value of patience is very beneficial to your life, and that to cultivate patience has a lot of benefits, including greater self-control over how you liaise and interact with other people and that by being patient stressful situations can be more easily resolved. It is important however, to realise that patience is a character value that does not come naturally to most of us and we may need a lot of willpower to improve our own character value of patience

Most of us rush around all day. We get up, rush to get ready to go to work or school, and even when we get back home we rush around doing other things before going to bed - often exhausted! We need to step back, take a break, even if only for a few minutes, have a cup of tea, relax, think of other things and improve your willpower to have more patience.

Judith Orloff MD in her blog article 'The Power of Patience' states that frustration is a key problem in our lives and recommends the practice of patience can be helped by purposefully standing in queues and filling the waiting time with positive action and thoughts.

There is, of course, much going on in all our lives, work, school, family, financial issues to mention just a few; but many of us also have dreams of something special we would like to achieve or do. Take that short break time to think about your dreams and how you might work towards achieving them. You will be surprised at how relaxed it will make you feel 'to think outside the box', even though the 'dream' is far from being achieved yet.

As for current issues, which often preoccupy so much of our time and energy, write lists and keep them handy e.g. 'Family'; 'Finances'; 'Studies' etc. Under each heading make a list starting with urgent, small issues first, down to the biggest problem at the bottom. As you solve or achieve items on the list you can cross them off, and you will then realise you are getting closer to solving the big issues. If done on a daily basis it can be very satisfying to see most things you wanted to do during the day actually completed and crossed off the list.

Enough to say "Yes, it's been a good day."

Patience with Family

'Patience with family is love, patience with others is respect'
Quote attributed to Ritu Ghatourey, female Indian author (details unknown)

It is sometimes easier to have patience with colleagues rather than family and people who are close to you. It is often challenging and difficult to have patience with relatives, including children; but in the family environment patience is very important.

We have all had occasions when you say something very simple and the other person takes it a different way and tempers flare; or the children interrupt you or demand your attention when you are in the middle of something else. Being patient in situations like this often leads to the other person or child learning a valuable lesson from you about how to behave towards other people.

Especially with children, they may often have to learn patience as they wait for you to complete the current job that they may have interrupted. That does not mean you ignore them, you just take a moment to advise them that you can attend to their need shortly and give them some sort of time factor (as soon as possible) as to when you will be free to give them your whole attention. Patience is a very important character value to use at times like this, and often means that you actually think more about the other person or child than yourself.

Patience with your spouse or partner is also important to maintain a healthy, loving relationship. Because of work and family responsibilities, often including sharing child care, quality time with your partner may be limited. It is very important to plan and arrange some spare time so that both of you can sit down together, preferably once a week, or even once a month, to discuss personal and family issues and sort out any problems that may have arisen. My son and his wife have some of this quality time together every Friday round their kitchen table, to discuss family and personal issues, and I feel sure that is one reason why their marriage is so stable. Your words can encourage others, but if used in anger or frustration may cause a fight. By planning together, unity is more likely and quarrels avoided.

Hopefully, with some of the suggestions in this chapter your life will become more calm and productive if lack of patience or hasty anger is a problem. However, you also need to be aware of what issues 'try your patience' and cause tension to rise. It happens to all of us at times and I am sure you have experienced the same. Can you define who or what 'tries your patience? How do you deal with it? Do you 'count to ten' or take a few deep breaths before responding?

Remember too, that it may be beneficial to put the matter aside for a while, actually walk away from confrontation, and resolve the issue at another time.

Also, remember the old saying – 'a soft answer turns away wrath'. Responding to a problem in a quiet manner will solve more issues successfully rather than resulting in quarrels and anger. One example of this is Aesop's Fable 'The North Wind and the Sun' where gentle persuasion is more effective than harsh action.

Patience in the Workplace

Teamwork is necessary to achieve the aims of any organisation. Most groups or companies will have policies for employees to follow so that the aims of the company or group are achieved. Policy aims cannot be achieved overnight.

The team will be made up of men and women with different characters and commitments. Patience is a key part in getting a group to work together for the common good, whether it is a community group, an established business or a government organisation.

1) Right leadership is important, of course.

2) Regular meetings to discuss progress and problems are needed. 3) Line management is also important, so that issues can be passed and discussed, up as well as down, throughout the organisation.

However, it is patience that plays such an important part in a family or any successful group or organisation.

1) Patience with each other.

2) Patience when working towards aims and objectives.

3) Patience to ensure the end goal is achieved.

HAVE PATIENCE

"There are three things to managing - The first is to have patience. The second is to be patient and the third most important secret is patience."

Chuck Tanner; 1928 -2011; American Baseball Player

Quote taken from ThinkExist.com

Change the World?

Can Patience help to change the world?

If there was more patience in the world there would be less anger, and hopefully people would first discuss matters rather than start arguing and fighting before thinking problems through to find answers. Of course, patience alone cannot solve all problems. Humans and the world are very complicated and diverse.

Some of our other character values, as well as patience, can be very useful to help change the world, for example, 'Forgiveness' and 'Caring' are needed in far greater amounts than currently seen, to help solve the world's problems. Also, we live in a computer age, where most people want the latest gadget. Do we appreciate the wonders of modern communication and entertainment? - All inventions are the result of someone patiently creating new ideas.

Do we appreciate all the good things in our lives? Many other people need to wait patiently for others to help them with problem solving and personal care.

CAN YOU CHANGE THE WORLD?

Links to Nature

"Adopt the pace of nature, her secret is patience". Ralph Waldo Emerson, 1803-1882, American Poet, Lecturer & Essayist

Next time that you eat an apple, have a thought about how long it took to grow, and the stages it went through to get into your hand. We all know that you can't eat fruit blossom, you have to wait for nature to take its course and in due season the fruit will be ready!

The same as when you plant a seed in your garden, the seed needs to be cared for if you want the best results. That is, the seed must be planted in the correct environment, watered, 'fed' and protected. Then you just have to have patience and let nature take its time and you will be rewarded with the 'fruit of your labour.'

It is the same with life. It takes time and patience to reach your chosen goal, to teach children about life and personal values, to overcome set-backs and deal with personal issues. Allow time for life's problems, plan well, look at problems from different angles, and be prepared to change the plan when necessary.

HAVE PATIENCE and you will see good results.

Patience is a Virtue

There is no doubt that patience is a virtue. We are not born with patience, but it can be nurtured and cultivated over time. Patience is usually acquired more as you gain maturity, because a lot of inner strength is required, but children also need to be encouraged to be patient.**(6)**

How can we gain more patience?

- Understand that everyone is different and with various life problems.
- Look at yourself and understand your own actions, then you can realise the best way to solve your problems.
- Once you have mastered your own problems you can see more clearly why other people react the way that they do, and you will be more aware of how to respond to them effectively.

- Listen to others point of view, and discuss differences openly, so understanding the actual problem can aid discussion and lead to possible resolution.
- The old adage of 'counting to ten' when presented with problems is an excellent way to use patience to give you a chance to review the situation and respond appropriately.

That simple task of 'counting to ten' or taking a short period to review the situation you are faced with, rather than jumping straight into an argument or worse, is the core of patience.

Patience is a virtue as well as an important character value. Are you prepared to improve your own level of patience? Patience is so important in our day and age for your own personal growth and enjoyment of life.

Patience Quotations

"How poor are those without patience! What wound did ever heal but by degrees?"

William Shakespeare, 1564- 1616; English Dramatist, Playwright and Poet.

"Genius is only a greater aptitude for patience."

George-Louis Leclerc de Buffon, !707-1788, French naturalist devoted to science.

"The key to everything is patience. You get the chicken by hatching the egg, not by smashing it open". Arnold H. Glasow, 1905 -1998, American humourist.

"Patience can't be acquired overnight. It is just like building up a muscle. Every day you need to work on it."

Eknath Easwaran, 1910-1999, Indian born Spiritual Leader, Translator and author of books on meditation.

“Patience and time do more than strength or passion.”

Jean de La Fontaine, 1621-1695; French poet and writer of fables.

"Commitment in
the face of conflict
produces character."

ZIG ZIGLA

CHAPTER 6

Do you think self-control is an
important character value?

How would you rate your own level of self-control?

What area of self-control is most important to you?

SELF-CONTROL

Self-control is just that - control of your own emotions and behaviour.

Especially how you talk to, and respond to others.

It also includes:-

- Listening rather than lecturing.
- Giving rather than demanding.
- Caring rather than lack of interest.

Self-control is a character value that you have to learn and work on all the time to be maintained at a high level. It is however, the basis of a good character and well worth achieving

"Prudent, cautious self-control is wisdom's root."

Robert Burns; 1759—1796; National Poet of Scotland

Quote from ThinkExist.com

Self-Discipline

An important part to ensure your own self-control is also to have self-discipline.

By this we mean knowing how to delegate your time to different sections of your life. It is mainly about 'time management' – how you manage and plan your time to improve yourself physically, emotionally and spiritually. This is not always easy, especially if you live a busy life with several different responsibilities. Personally, I know this to be one of my own problems with self-control, in that I may get distracted by other people when in the middle of a project.

In fact, time management is an essential part of self-discipline and self-control.

Time management is especially important if you have regular employment or if you are studying for a course or exam, and would include:-

- Getting to work or class on time i.e. being punctual.
- Ensuring that you complete assignments within the designated time.
- Time with your family and loved ones, to relax and enjoy each other's company, and to discuss and sort out issues together.
- Time for social events or leisure time.

However, self-discipline does cover other areas of your life as well as time.

Your physical needs should also be considered:-

- Are you caring enough for your body?

- Are you eating the proper food?
- Taking sufficient exercise?
- Also avoiding too much alcohol?

Your health is so important to maintaining a happy life both for yourself and your family.

Spiritual needs also have an important part in many lives:-

Have the self-discipline to follow your own faith, while allowing others, in this diverse society, to follow their own. After all, we are in the end, all heading the same way!

Know Yourself

Self-control can be equated with self-awareness or knowing more about how you behave under different circumstances.

- What makes you upset?
- What makes you angry?
- What things do you dislike?

When you are aware of these things you can have more self-control over how you react when such instances occur. Keeping lists of your likes and dislikes can help you be more aware of what area of self-control you need to work on.

The importance of your tongue and how you speak to others cannot be over emphasized. So much damage is done by loose talk, gossip and unnecessary rude or negative remarks.

Always think before you make any adverse remarks, there must be a real reason for making such comments, maybe to give advice to the other person.

Give positive remarks or comments before bringing up negative issue, by doing so:-

- You will improve relationships.
- Make the other person feel more positive.
- You will always get better results, no matter the circumstances.
- Remember too, that old proverb - 'a soft answer turns away wrath'.

"Your chances of success in any undertaking can always be measured by your belief in yourself." Robert Collier; 1885–1950; American motivational author

Quote taken from ThinkExist.com

Have you thought about which Character values you already possess? Also, what character values you would like to improve / attain?

Gaining Self-Control

There are a lot of pressures within our families as well as from society as a whole to 'keep up to date', especially as technology advances so quickly. An important part of gaining self-control is to actually think of yourself and what you want from life instead of 'following the herd' or being pressured into being the same as everyone else.

You have been given the ability to make choices, you have free will to say 'yes' or 'no' to life's events. It is known that individual circumstances can affect your decisions, in particular the time factors involved in achieving the change that leads to self-control, but the important thing is to want and work towards that change.

Make two lists of what you class as your best character value and those character values you would like to explore or possess, and list the steps you believe you need to take to achieve your goal. Detailed lists are very helpful; keep them where you can see them daily e.g. in your diary or on your mirror. The satisfaction of crossing off any goal as it is achieved is immense and it does not have to be a major item.

TAKE LITTLE STEPS AT A TIME

Financial Control

Finances and money issues take up a great part of our lives, and in the current world control of your individual financial matters is essential for your stability and growth. Part of self-control is knowing how to manage your finances effectively and then you will be a step closer to self-respect and self-control. Concentrate first on what you need, rather than what you want.

It may not be easy, as you may already be a victim of the financial glut that was encouraged in past years. Even if you are in debt now, take control, get professional help to clear the debts and you will have a greater feeling of being in control of your own life, rather than worrying about how other people or institutions may affect your future.

Teach your children the difference between 'want' and 'need'. There is a lot of peer pressure and advertising in modern society encouraging unnecessary desire and greed. Also, encourage your children to save some of their pocket money. They will enjoy the result of doing that, while also learning about the cost of living, and it will be a start towards their own discipline and self-control.

Helping Others

Once you have gained some self-control it becomes easier to help other people to do the same thing. But it is not something that can be taught, the person involved has to want to gain self-control themselves; you will only be able to guide and advise them on their journey of self-development.

This is where setting an example has such a good effect. When others see how you use self-control under trying and difficult circumstances they want to be able to do the same.

Here again, the way you talk to others has an important effect. Encouragement and giving advice work a lot better than lectures and negative remarks. Always find some positive remarks to say before discussing problems or issues and try to end the conversation on a positive note as well.

Self-control for Children

Helping our children gain self-control can only have a beneficial effect. Parenting is not always easy but Kidshealth.org have some excellent advice about teaching your child self-control depending on the child's age.

The Bottom Line

It is up to you, and only you, to gain self-control of your attitude, behaviour and the way your life continues. To know your own good and bad character traits and to gain self-control of your behaviour and emotions can only be an advantage to your own physical, emotional and spiritual growth; but gaining self-control can take time; it is not an overnight event.

There may, also be some restrictions, due to the environment you currently live in, but that need not stop you from improving your own personality or character.

With self-control you become better parents and good leaders.

Become the person you want to be by improving your own character values, especially self-control, and you will find that your whole life will improve in a positive way.

Self-Control Quotations

"Confirm thy soul in self-control."

George Washington; 1732—1799; 1st US President 1789—97

"Most powerful is he who has himself in his own power."

Seneca, Roman Philosopher; mid-1st century AD.

"Your chances of success in any undertaking can always be measured by your belief in yourself." Robert Collier, 1885-1950; American motivational author.

"Self-confidence is the first requisite to great undertakings."

Samuel Johnson, 1709-1784; English Poet, Critic and Writer.

"Man cannot live without self-control."

Issac Bashevia Singer, 1904-1991; Polish-born American Writer.

"Prudent cautious self-control is wisdom's root."

Robert Burns, 1759-1796; National poet of Scotland.

"Any fool can criticize, condemn and complain, but it takes character and self-control to be understanding and forgiving."

Dale Camegie, 1888-1955; American Lecturer and Author.

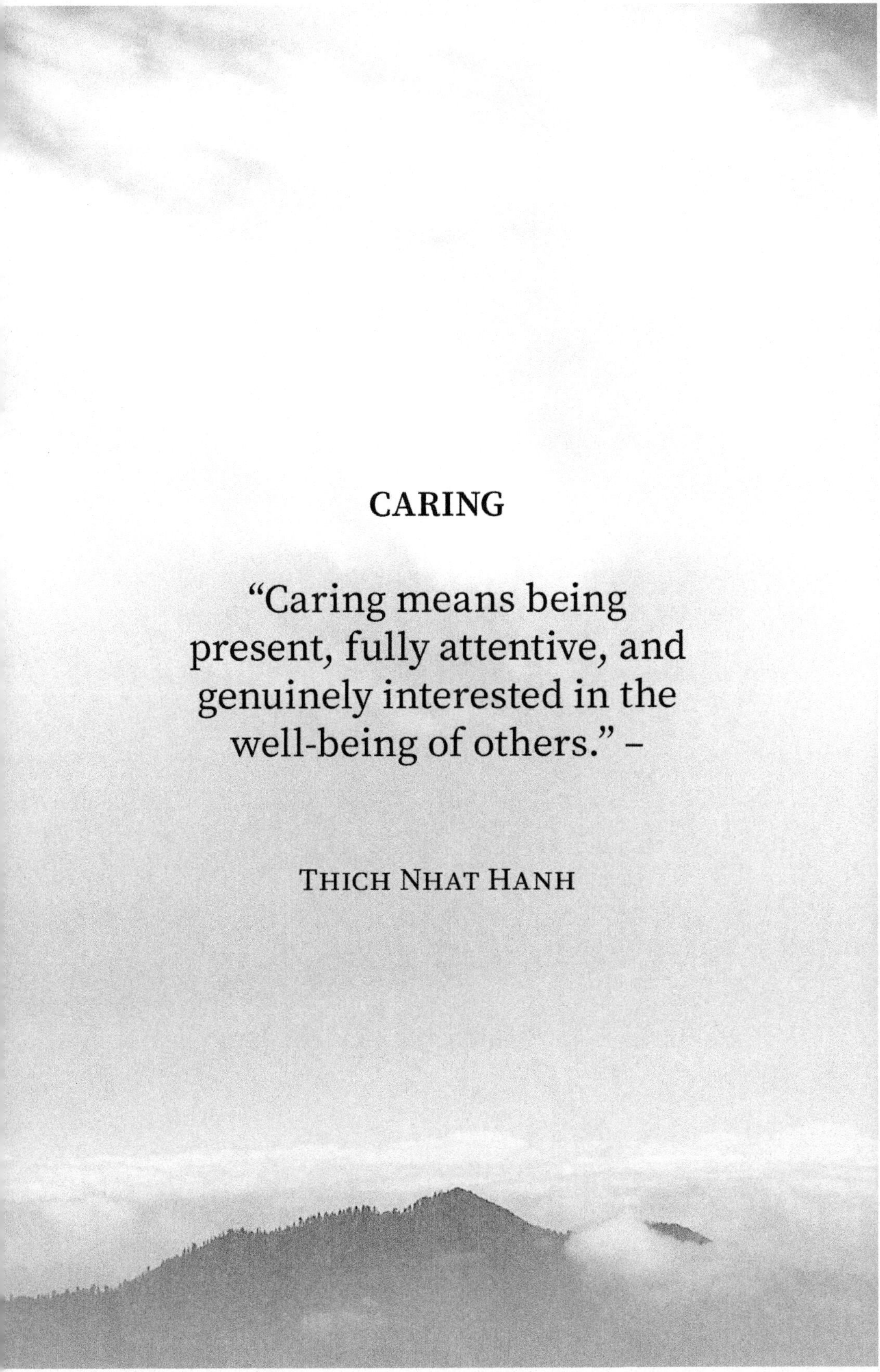

CARING

"Caring means being present, fully attentive, and genuinely interested in the well-being of others." –

THICH NHAT HANH

CHAPTER 7

Do you have a family that you care about, or
that care for you? Then you are blessed.

Remember those who are alone or feel lonely.

What happens to those people who are homeless?

How do they eat? How do they
manage their toilet needs?

So many families in refugee camps. How can we care?

CARING

In simple terms caring is about thinking of and helping other people; also being aware of other people's need, being compassionate, having understanding of and empathy with different groups of people.

In the present unsettled financial environment, most adults are preoccupied with job security and financial worries. When a person is preoccupied with problems, it is difficult to think about other things. That is the time to remember our first character value— 'Appreciation' - to think about and be thankful for all the good things in your life. Then you begin to think of other people worse off than yourself and to think about how you might help them.

'To care is to show humanness - care is the one virtue that most closely resembles love'

Caring is a small word but can have huge results:-

- To care is to express humanness.
- A caring person is outward focused and has a positive attitude.
- A caring person is considerate, kind, compassionate and generous.
- A caring person will take into account how decisions, words and actions are likely to affect other people.
- Those who are helped feel appreciated and more important.
- Those who are helped will find their lives improved in a positive manner.
- Society improves in a positive way when people care about each other.
- People who care also find that their lives improve in a positive way.

Caring does not have to be a major event. 'Little things mean a lot':-

- Helping someone across the road.
- Giving up your bus or train seat for an elderly or disabled person.
- Smiling more at people. Smiling is 'infectious' – If someone smiles at you then you would naturally smile back at them. Smiling releases endorphins which improve your own well-being.
- Hugs and handshakes express warmth and caring, both for children and adults, leading to better trust and discussion.

Children—how do you show your mummy or daddy that you care for them?

Do you help in the house - give them hugs? **HELPING OTHERS IS CARING**

Caring for Yourself

Your own health is very important especially if you have other people to care for. You need to take care of yourself, so that you stay healthy and well. That includes taking enough exercise and a healthy diet.

Remember:

- Try to eat 5 portions a day of fruit and vegetables.
- Some time to relax and renew your mental energy is also very important. Get out to a park, - enjoy nature; read a good book or consider meditation.
- Treat yourself occasionally to something special; a trip out to somewhere that interests you, a sports event, the theatre, musical or arts event. You will enjoy the outing more if you take a friend or companion with you.
- Everyone seems to dress casually these days, with formal wear only for special occasions. However, make sure your clothes are clean and neat, and consider wearing light or bright colours to give more positive vibes to those around you.

Caring within your Family

Are you part of a happy family unit, with love and affectionate care at its centre? You have so much to be thankful for. A united family works as a team, children helping with chores and listening to their parent's advice;

parents caring for their children's health, education and happiness. Hopefully you allow family discussions too, so that your children feel comfortable with telling you about any problems they may have.

However, even in an ideal family situation, things change, problems occur, and sometimes family groups even break up. Why?

Well, we are all individuals, with our own thoughts and ideas. Our parents each grew up in different family units. Sometimes our parents do not realize how incompatible they are until they have been together for a while. Alternatively, too many problems and stresses can cause quarrels, rifts and family break-up. Family units should ideally be permanent, but if your family unit does break up, don't blame yourself or your parents. You are there in the family because your parents once had a good relationship. Remember the good times and positive events and maintain family contact as much as possible.

Love, care and empathy are the important character values that can carry you through tough times as well as good times.

Caring for those in need

DUTY OF CARE

It is our duty to care for others, not to avoid them, especially when they need us.

Leadership, whether at home, work or in groups involves being purposely engaged in the lives of other 'team' members, to ensure unity and progress.

CARE FOR EACH OTHER

- A big part of maturity is the ability to think and care about someone else besides oneself.
- Be 'we' minded not 'me' minded.
- Being kind to others is the most important thing we can do in this lifetime.
- Helping others without a selfish motive enriches your own life.
- Care about others – how they can be more positive about their lives. We hurt ourselves and others by negative thoughts and actions.
- Giving helpful advice to those that ask for our help – signposting those who need help to groups / agencies that may be more helpful in their particular circumstances.

There are many different ways you can care for those in need.

- Friends may need to talk in confidence about problems.
- Neighbours may need a helping hand with jobs or shopping.
- There are numerous charities that need financial help.

Choose a charity that interests you. Find out more about the charity. Think about arranging a sponsored event to raise money. Sponsored events can be fun as well as profitable. Sponsored events also raise awareness about the work of the charity.

For some people caring for others may seem like a burden, but in fact, care is the counterbalance that gives life its vibrancy and authenticity. Be proud of the care and help that you give to others. It is however, advisable to give help that is urgently needed before giving further advice or signposting the person to other agencies.

As part of caring we need to remind children the importance of the following points:-

- Always tell your parents what you are doing and where you plan to go - get their permission.
- If your friends talk to you in confidence, then keep that confidence, unless you think your friend is in danger of harm. Then you must tell your parents.
- If you know your neighbours need help, discuss with your parents so they can ensure the help is appropriate and safe for you to do.

Empathy

EMPATHY is a very important word, and is part of caring for each other. Empathy actually means:- 'The ability to share and understand another's feelings', such as 'stepping into someone else's shoes' that is - you are more aware of why people behave and act as they do.

It is a very big subject, worthy of a whole lecture on its own.

Empathy is a key to peace. If you understand why a person says or does the things they do, you are less likely to be offended by their actions or words, and more likely to reply in a positive or appropriate way. Therefore, talking to and listening to other people is important.

How about having discussion groups in your school or at work, maybe at lunch times? Ask questions, learn about your colleagues and school mates. You may make some new long-term friends. At least, you will learn to understand more about each other.

Caring for the Environment

We are all beginning to realise the importance of the environment, and to know what items can be recycled. The more we recycle items the less of our natural resources we need to use. So we are caring for the environment.

What do we mean by 'recycling'? Well, for example, used paper, empty tins and bottles can be prepared and reused to make the same product. Food scraps and garden waste can be prepared to be produce fertilizer for agriculture.

Most councils now encourage recycling and will give out special containers for items that can be recycled. If you do not use these services already do contact your local council for details of their recycling facilities. When we recycle tins and bottles, we not only use less of the natural resources, we also preserve the earth! Tins, bottles and plastic do not decompose, so the less empty tins and bottles that are buried as rubbish the better it is for the earth. Plastic items are a more serious problem as the accumulation of waste plastic is now causing serious environmental problems on land and sea and affecting wild life. Please do care about the environment and ensure your waste products are disposed of safely. A little care can make a lot of difference to the environment

ALSO:-

Remember to turn off lights and electrical equipment when they are not in use.

Ensure taps are turned off tight. A lot of water is wasted by dripping taps.

Caring for Pets

If you have pets, it is very important that you understand how to care for them properly. You need to read books, research or ask a pet shop owner how to care for the pet you want to keep.

What type of shelter or 'home' do they need? How do you keep their cage, tank or basket clean? What should your pet eat and how often? Where do you buy their food? Animals, birds and fish all have different needs.

So before having a pet you need to know that you have the time and the means to care for the pet. Basically, the bigger the pet the more care it needs; e.g. dogs need grooming and exercise every day, whereas a fish needs little care, so long as their tank water is clean. House pets, such as dogs and cats, like to be shown affection by being petted and stroked.

Please think about these things and discuss it with your family before getting a pet.

Happy pet keeping.

Summary

We all possess the character value of caring to a certain degree, usually within the family environment. Improving or extending this important character value will definitely improve society. How can you increase your own caring character value?

Caring Quotations

'The greatest disease in the west is not tuberculosis or leprosy, it is being unwanted, unloved and uncared for'.

Mother Theresa, 1910 – 1997, Roman Catholic Nun and Missionary, Nobel Peace Prize 1997, Founder of the Missionaries of Charity

'Kindness in words creates confidence.' Lao-Tzu, Ancient Chinese Philosopher

'Kindness is a language that the deaf can hear and the blind can read.'

Mark Twain, 1935 – 1910, American Author and Humourist.

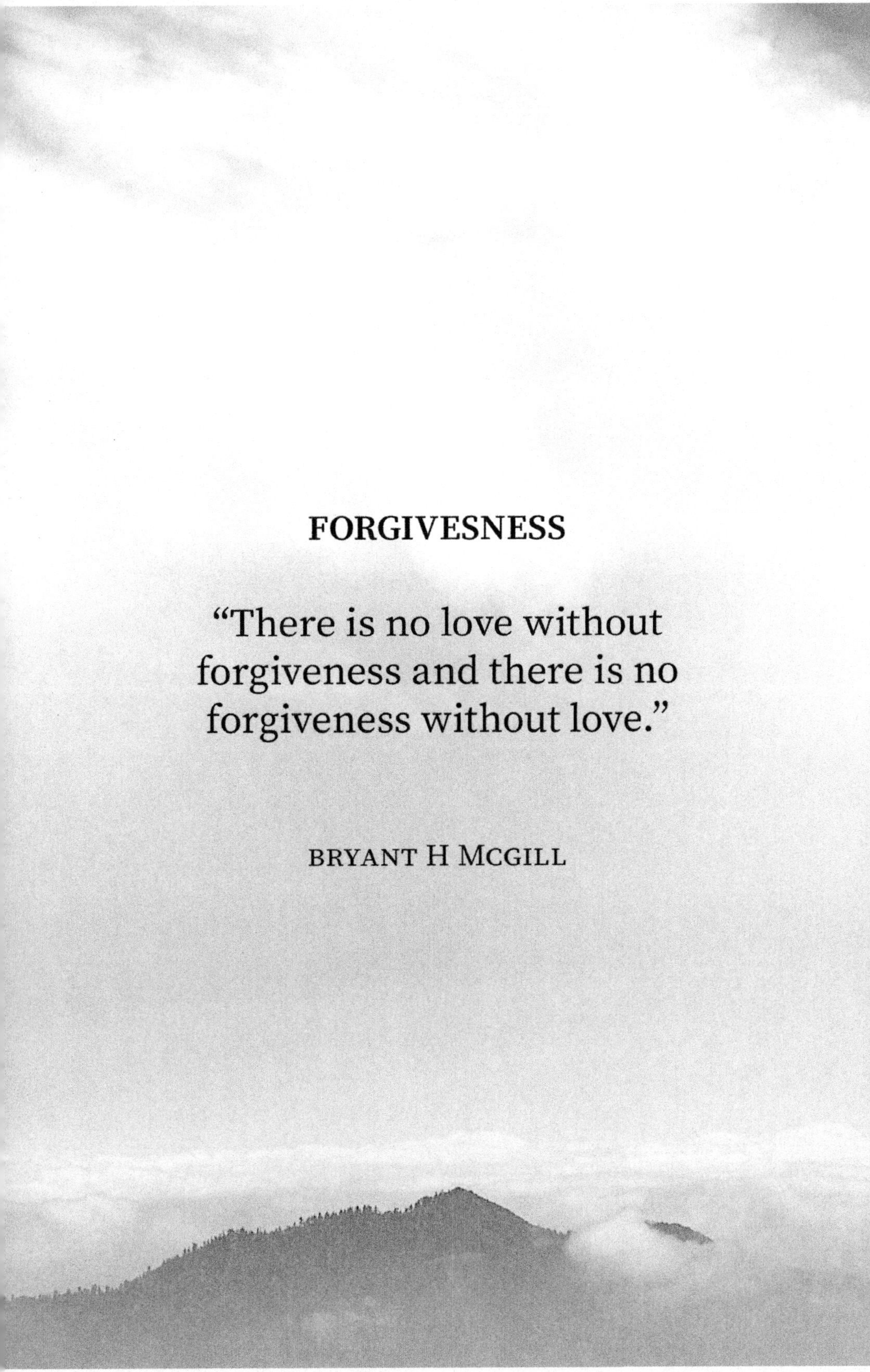

FORGIVESNESS

"There is no love without forgiveness and there is no forgiveness without love."

BRYANT H MCGILL

CHAPTER 8

Are there parts of your life you regret,
wish you could go back and change?

Events or people you find it difficult to forgive?

Are there people you need to ask for forgiveness?

Let's try to shine some light on
this very difficult subject

FORGIVENESS

The word 'Forgiveness' is a verb meaning to forgive, to pardon, to cease to feel resentment to another. Forgiveness is a very difficult subject for many people to think about, but this particular character value is very important.

FORGIVENESS is a two-part subject:-

- Asking for forgiveness
- Giving forgiveness

Forgiveness is not an easy subject to discuss or debate. There are lots of strong feelings about what is right and wrong, and about self worth.

We have all lost our temper sometime, saying something that we immediately or later regret. All are guilty of some transgression big or small and we all need forgiveness. Likewise, we often feel anger or resentment against someone who has said or done something to offend us and are reluctant to let the anger and resentment go.

REMEMBER :- **NONE OF US IS PERFECT**

AESOP'S FABLE – The Two Bags, this simple tale reminds us to look at our own faults before criticizing others.

Possible causes of friction

Stress

Modern day life can be stressful with its different financial, emotional and physical problems everywhere:-

- Many people are losing their jobs through the current financial climate.
- Sudden changes in life style can be difficult to accept and adjust to.
- Stress brings tension; and tension leads to over reacting and quick loss of temper and often un-necessary quarrels.
- Stress is probably the main cause of domestic quarrels.

AIMS TO PREVENT STRESS WITHIN THE FAMILY:-

Be thankful for positive events.

Try to take some quiet time together.

Don't blame each other.

Sit down and discuss your domestic/personal issues together.

Discuss and agree together what needs to be done to maintain the family unity; taking into consideration the changing circumstances.

Be truthful. It takes two to quarrel.

REMEMBER –

- A quiet answer often stops a quarrel, and will lead to discussion, rather than a fight.
- We need to know our own faults and improve on them before we start to criticise other people.

Anger, Fear, and Hate

This controversial heading is necessary, because we need to acknowledge that most quarrels and fights are caused by one or more of the above.

- Quarrels can be caused by anger, stress, or reactions to what someone else has done or said - leading to replies of verbal or physical abuse, then tempers flare, and things go from bad to worse.
- Some people react through fear, maybe from some past bad experiences, or poor family history, e.g. lack of proper parental support or love.
- People who hate something or someone take their issues further, leading to serious fights, violence and terrorism.
- Some people surround themselves with a 'protective wall'. They won't let other people get close for fear of rejection or being hurt again; or often the tongue is used as a weapon (blaming others) to keep people, even family, at a distance.

- In our current culture of fear, many people carry other weapons, knives and guns to 'protect themselves'.
- Verbal abuse is probably the most common cause of misunderstanding and quarrels. Swearing at, or calling someone by a derogatory name is one example of verbal abuse.
- False accusations and gossip also cause so many problems; or someone may say something which is misinterpreted by another, leading to misunderstandings and quarrels.

THINK BEFORE YOU ACT - WE ARE ALL HUMAN.

Helpful Tips:-

- Avoid starting a sentence with 'You always.......'.
- No -one is perfect, avoid name calling and labelling people.

Our Tongues

That little muscle in our mouths that helps us to chew and swallow food, is one of the biggest trouble makers in the world.

Without a tongue we could not talk, therefore there would be no verbal abuse, swearing, or quarrels! What a wonderful thought!

But it is important that we do communicate with each other, learn more about our neighbours, discuss differences and learn from each other, rather than create barriers.

Language and speech, are part of our living culture. We need to remember that some words may have a different meaning to people of other cultures. One example of this are the words 'thank you' and 'please' so important to one culture, but expressed by other means in other cultures. Easy to discuss and learn - thus overcoming misunderstandings and resentment.

ANGER IS ONLY ONE LETTER AWAY FROM DANGER

THINK BEFORE YOU ARGUE.

Asking for Forgiveness

Asking for forgiveness is not easy.

The most important thing is that you realise you have done something wrong/or offended someone, and are genuinely sorry.

How you apologise or make amends is really up to you...... a card, a letter, a small present, an offer of help. Make an appointment; go with a friend......

There are many different ways to apologise, and many suitable cards in shops that you can buy to send as a first move to your apology.

If other people know about the issue, you need to inform them that you are making amends, thereby putting a stop to misunderstandings and unnecessary gossip.

APOLOGISING IS A VERY POSITIVE ACT.

There are occasions when the person to whom you want to apologise, feels unable to forgive you. There may be several reasons for this, including deep hurt by your actions/words. Try again to apologise in a different way.

If the person you offended feels unable to forgive you after your two attempts to apologise, there is not much you can do about it, except to show by your future actions that you meant no harm and are truly sorry for the original offence.

Forgiving

Anyone can hold a grudge, but it takes a person with character to forgive.

When you forgive you release yourself from a powerful burden.

It is not easy to forgive someone who has offended or hurt you; but if that person comes to you with a genuine apology, is it not better to accept that apology, 'forgive and forget' and start afresh?

What is important is:-

- That you discuss the past openly with the person who is asking for your forgiveness, so they understand how their actions or words hurt or offended you.
- Also, **you** can set the ground rules for a new relationship, whether the person who offended you can still be part of your life or not. If you need time to think about this, after acknowledging the apology, you could ask to meet again at a later date to discuss how you can both move forward.

We do realise that some offences are very minor, like a broken plate or favourite ornament, - other offences can be very serious, like defamation of character or physical harm. Whatever the offence, if you can find it within yourself to forgive, you will be surprised at the feeling of release and peace you will find. Forgiving does benefit the giver as well as the recipient.

Do you need to forgive someone? Do you need to ask for forgiveness? These actions may be difficult, but well worth the effort.

Forgiveness Quotations

'The weak can never forgive. Forgiveness is the attribute of the strong.'

Mahatma Gandhi 1869 – 1948, Indian Philosopher, internationally esteemed for his doctrine of non-violent protests.

'Forgiveness does not change the past, but it does enlarge the future.'

Paul Boese 1923 -1976, American Businessman and writer.

'We achieve inner health only through forgiveness- the forgiveness not only of others but also of ourselves.'

Joshua Loth Liebman 1907-1948 American Rabbi and best-selling author.

'To err is human, to forgive is devine' Alexander Pope 1688-1744 18th Century English Poet

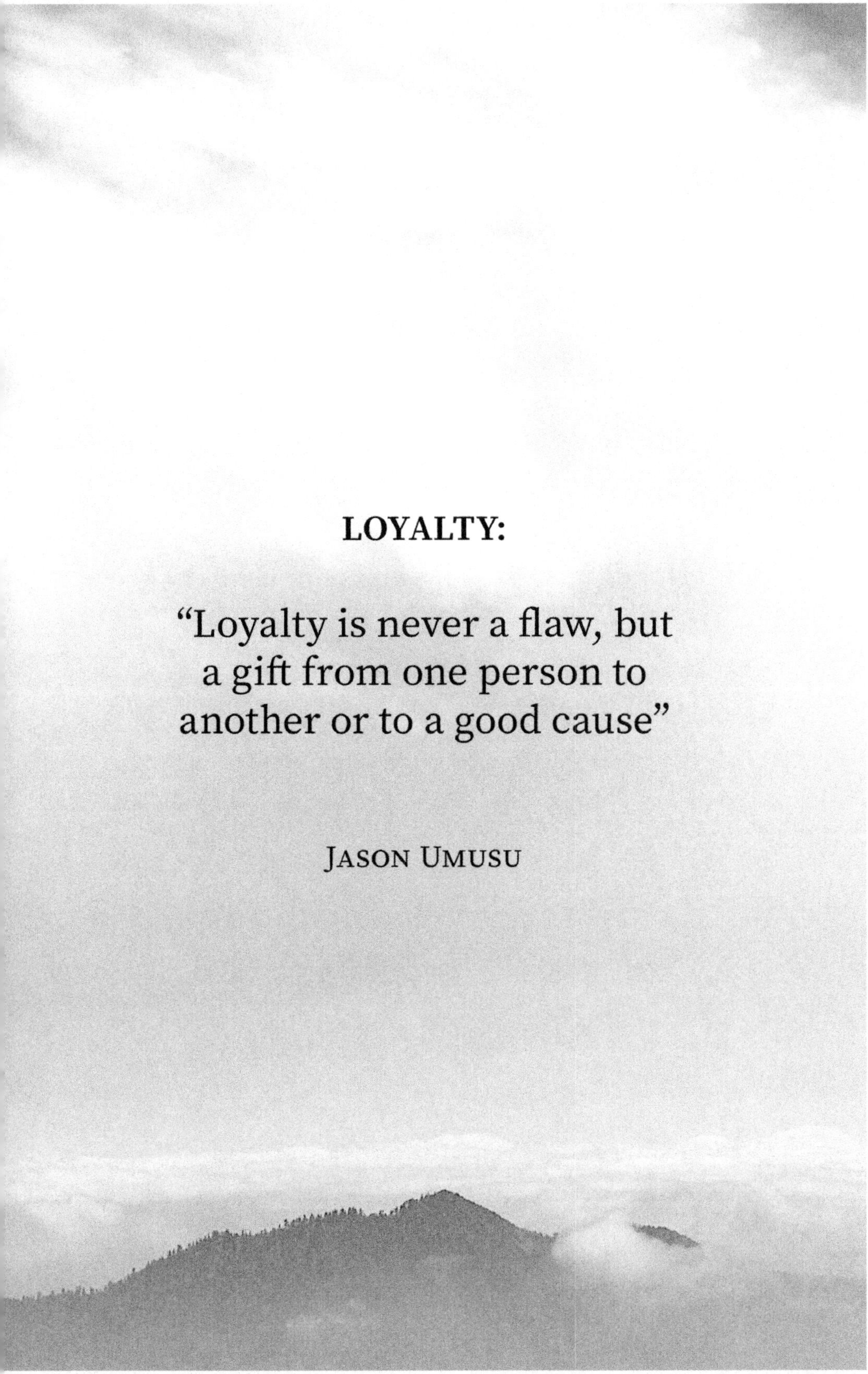

LOYALTY:

"Loyalty is never a flaw, but
a gift from one person to
another or to a good cause"

JASON UMUSU

CHAPTER 9

What does the word loyalty mean to you?
Is there loyalty within your family?
Are you loyal to your friends and colleagues and the country you live in?

LOYALTY

Webster's Concise Edition dictionary gives the meaning of Loyalty as allegiance, constancy, devotion, faithfulness, fealty, fidelity and patriotism. These are powerful words, worthy to be part of your own character; and also for in-depth discussion.

'We live in a world where selfishness seems to be the rule of the day, and personal gain the objective of most relationships and endeavours. One of the most honorable character traits a person can develop is the ability to be loyal, whether to family, friends, an employer, or clubs and organisations to which they belong.'

This quote, from an excellent article on loyalty by the organisation Virtue First Foundation, based in USA, identifies, in its first sentence, a major problem with today's society.

Loyalty is important—it is the 'glue' that binds families, groups and communities together. Loyalty can be between just two people, amongst friends, family, a specialised group, workforce or within a huge community.

What is important is that:-

- Loyalty has a place in the home, within the family, in the workplace as well as faith and social groups.
- For loyalty to be a character value it must work towards the good welfare of others.
- Your actions benefit not only the group or person that you are loyal to, but others outside the group as well.
- Loyalty ties in with other character values such as caring, honesty, respect and responsibility.

Each of these areas will be discussed further.

Loyalty to your Family

'Blood makes you related, LOYALTY makes you FAMILY'

Unknown source

The core of societies is the family unit.

Within a happy, united family loyalty plays a big part.

Ideally the family unit consists of loving adults and children. The parents supporting each other in caring for their children to the best of their ability, but always teaching family values of loyalty, respect and teamwork.

Teamwork, that is:-

1. Working together on family issues and problems.

2. Trusting each other to follow through on family agreements.
3. Loving but disciplined care by the adults with the children learning, understanding and keeping to 'family rules'.

All these add up to loyalty within the family.

There are always 'ups and downs' in our lives and more so in family units where people with difference characters live together. This is where it is important for the parents to discuss and decide on 'house rules' together so that they are both united when discussing discipline, teamwork and loyalty with their children.

Part of this, also, is for the children to feel confident of their parent's love and that they feel able to discuss any problem, or misunderstanding, that they may have with their parents, and also be able to ask their parents questions as the need arises.

Of course, there are also one parent families due to various reasons, including bereavement and separation. Loyalty within such family groups is even more important and can be fostered by the parent ensuring they spend time with their child to have fun, as well as making the child feel that they are needed.

Loyalty to Friends & Colleagues

Loyalty sounds a very intense word, but in fact it's not.

It is mainly about caring what happens to those people close to you and in your local environment.

Once outside your home environment your relationships can become very diverse. We meet friends, go to school or college and work with people from all nationalities. In the context of your friends and colleagues, loyalty is again about discussion, setting rules or policies and working as a team.

Discussion is very important for you to put across your own opinions, sort out what is relevant and agree on common terms (rules or policies). Loyalty to your colleagues involves ensuring through teamwork that the terms or policies agreed between yourselves are complied with. These may be by mutual agreement or written down as a policy, which in the workplace may even have legal implications.

In addition, with friends it is the same - nothing may be written down, but you all agree where you will go, when and what time and have some sort of plan as to what you will all do. Complying with these plans is being loyal to your friends.

Loyalty to your country

Loyalty to the country you live in is as important as loyalty to your birth country – and this may well be the same country, seeing that many people settle and have their families in more secure environments than where their forefathers originated from.

Humankind is currently fragmented like a broken mirror. People of different countries, clans, tribes, cultures and beliefs are scattered all over the world. If your birth country is different from where you decide to live, are your loyalties divided?

This is one reason why communication is so important - the need to understand each other, to be able to live together with our differences in peace.

Loyalty to the country you live in is vital. You live there, one presumes, for security, happiness and peace. By taking up your true role as a citizen of that country you improve yourself and the country you live in. Community groups that are open to all in the local area, help improve understanding, peace and loyalty between all people.

Citizenship

Citizenship goes hand-in hand with loyalty and you cannot discuss one without talking about the other. Part of being loyal to your country means that you are a 'good citizen' - that you know the laws of your country, abide by them and encourage others, especially the children, to be 'law-abiding citizens'.

Happily, citizenship is now part of the school's curriculum, and although the curriculum explains a lot about government and how people live and work together, loyalty and social responsibility are, hopefully, also be included in the discussions.

So what is citizenship all about? What makes one a good citizen?

From the point of view of this character value related topic we should perhaps think about how we behave towards each other.

Do we spend enough time finding out about our neighbours, their cultures and customs? Also to tell them about our own culture, of course? Would it be useful to initiate 'coffee mornings' amongst a few neighbours for example?

Citizenship is fostered by some of The Character Well's other character values: -

1) Appreciation for the benefits your government does supply,

2) Caring for others - even simple things like looking out for your elderly neighbours, or people who live alone.

3) Caring also includes encouraging community unity and empathy.

4) Honesty, in word and deeds.

5) Respect for other people's views and beliefs.

6) Taking responsibility for your own actions.

Communities are now very diverse, different cultures and faiths intermingled. Understanding this and learning to live together, in the same community, is vital to the peace, progress and stability of any country. You may like to encourage the character value of loyalty by taking a greater part in your local community.

However, in the end, it is everyone's individual action of being a 'law-abiding citizen' that will improve society and give our children a better future.

Other types of 'Loyalty'

Pets, especially dogs, can be very loyal to their owners, and only need rewarding with good care and affection.

Humans, however, even with their ability to reason, sometimes have 'misplaced or misguided loyalty'- that is, being loyal to groups and gangs that have ulterior motives and generally work outside the law. Crime and lies are the usual outcome of such misplaced loyalty.

Misplaced loyalty may give a personal feeling of power, but with that comes the fear both of your peers and the wider community.

Misplaced Loyalty is not of permanent value and often leads to harm for other people.

- Does your family know?
- What reputation do you want to have?
- What legacy do you want to leave?
- Is misplaced loyalty really worth it?

Let us work together towards greater and more positive loyalties.

Summary

Loyalty is important character value, important for your progress and the whole of society.

Are you prepared to improve your own character value of loyalty?

Loyalty Quotations

"Our loyalties must transcend our race, our tribe, our class, and our nation; and this means we must develop a world perspective".

Martin Luther King Jn. ; 1929-1968; American Civil Rights Leader and Baptist Minister

"Loyalty is still the same, whether it win or lose the game; true as a dial to the sun, although it is not shined upon." Samuel Butler, 1835-1902; English novelist, essayist and critic.

"An ounce of loyalty is worth a pound of cleverness."

Elbert Hubbard, 1856-1915; American editor, publisher and writer.

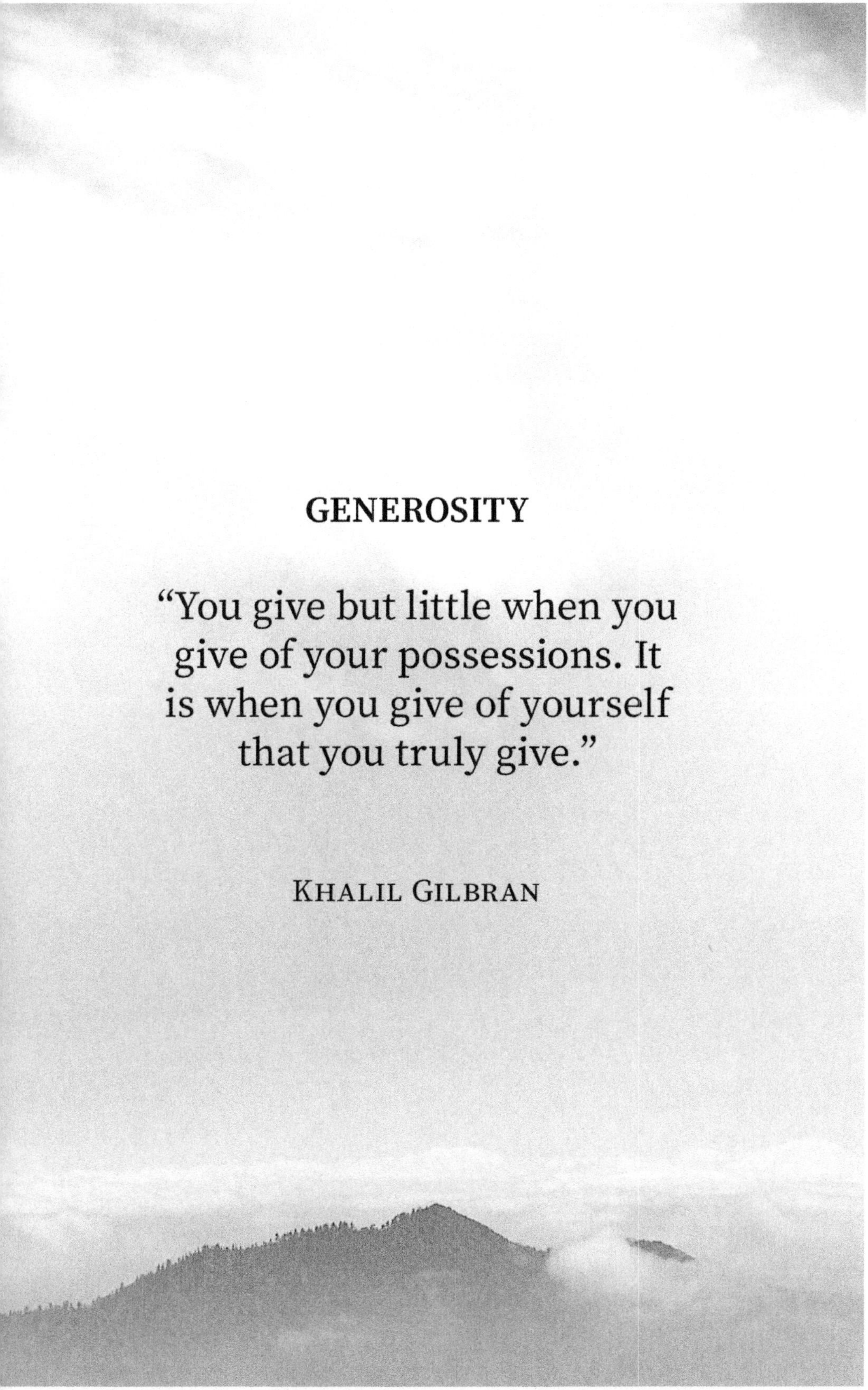

GENEROSITY

"You give but little when you give of your possessions. It is when you give of yourself that you truly give."

KHALIL GILBRAN

CHAPTER 10

Are we generous enough?
Is generosity about other things besides money?
How do you use the gifts you have?

GENEROSITY

What do we mean by GENEROSITY?

To most people it is about giving money to those in need; but there are many other things that we can be generous with our time, our care, our own knowledge and experience.

'Real generosity is doing something nice for someone who will never find out'.

Frank A Clark 1911– 1991

(The Country Parson Series)

Quote taken from ThinkExist.com.

Generosity benefits the giver as well as the recipient.

Generosity through Charity

Do you give donations?

It is good practice to donate money to charities, especially if there is one that you have a special interest in. Some people use direct debit to donate each month, others may give occasionally or when they receive an appeal letter. Others may donate secretly.

Charities, of course, rely on public donations to carry out their excellent work.

Have you ever worked as a volunteer?

If you are unable to give money to charities, you can always offer to help in some other way. Maybe you can sell their lottery tickets or work as a volunteer in a charity shop of your choice, or arrange a sponsored event to raise money for the charity.

If you are unsure which charity to help you need to contact your local Volunteer Centre for advice on all volunteer vacancies available.

Do you help with sponsored events?

There are many different types of sponsored events. They can be fun, as well as good community effort and can raise a lot of money for different causes.

Sponsored events can range from arranging a jumble or boot sale, to a major event like a fair with different rides and stalls or a show with popular artists taking part. These events may often gain money for charities by entrance ticket fees.

Some sponsored events involve running certain distances – like the Marathon. Such events involve the whole of society, and even people from other countries, adults, children and disabled people, all raising funds for the charity of their choice by their own efforts.

However, remember that sponsored events can be any fun event, a writing or a reading contest. Games and dances too. Use your imagination.

Small or big— Make fun a major part
of your sponsored charity event.

Generous with Our Time

Using your own time to care for, teach or help others is being generous with your time.

- Those who help at pensioner centres, volunteering to help with charity work, environmental work or rescue work—all are being generous with their time. They also, all play an important part by fostering a community atmosphere; people working together to help each other.
- Other people may give one-to-one care, help or teaching.
- Even something as simple as helping someone across the road, giving up your seat in the bus, giving someone directions, all involve giving, that is, being generous with your time.
- Teachers, of course give their knowledge as well as their time.

Whether it is a parent teaching values and discipline to their child, or how to cook fairy cakes; or a university lecturer teaching higher physics - and all teachers in between - we need to be grateful, that is, appreciate that they share their knowledge, talents and time with us.

Generous with Knowledge

We have all been given special gifts. Life, itself, is a gift. A gift we should be grateful for each day. Also, we all have special talents and various depth of knowledge that we can pass on to other people. Everything you do or say can be a lesson for someone else.

The way you behave in your life and towards others is an example, or lesson to others.

Apart from that, you may have specialised knowledge or talents that would be useful to other people studying or working in the same field. And of course, the children — our future ambassadors - are a fertile ground for all types of knowledge. We also need to teach them the correct way to use the things they learn.

All knowledge is good.

It is how you USE that knowledge that makes it good or evil.

Generous with Feelings

This is just a gentle reminder to be generous with your feelings; that it is important to value and show appreciation for the people in your life.

It is important to show your family that you care about them, and appreciate that they are part of your life. By doing this you are improving family unity and happiness.

It is a simple matter really, of giving regular praise and encouragement, and to be interested in what your family members are doing. A nice hug, a pat on the back or a handshake will show your pride in their achievements.

Children could occasionally send a 'Thank you' card to their Dad or Mum (you don't have to wait for Mother's or Father's Day), or offer to do something special to help in the house or garden.

Generous with Forgiveness

To forgive someone for something they have said or done to hurt or offend you, is not often very easy. However, forgiveness is a great act of generosity.

Whereas other acts of generosity come spontaneously, or are carried out because we care, forgiveness is a conscious act, and involves a lot of self-thought.

It is, however, well worth being generous with forgiveness. By forgiving you clear away masses of clogging thoughts that hang like cobwebs on your minds and prevent you from making more positive use of your life.

'To forgive is to set a prisoner free and discover that the prisoner was you.'

Lewis B Smedes, 1921-2002, American Christian Author

Summary

Generosity is an important character value. By recognizing the need of others and being generous with our time, efforts and money, you are taking an active part in the community and helping humanity in general. Therefore, people who are being generous to others, in any way, achieve a feeling of satisfaction and joy that they have used their gifts for positive purposes. This is so whether the gifts or talents are used in an open manner, as in teaching, or by secret donations.

Children can be generous by helping with small jobs at home, helping their brothers and sisters with reading and writing, sharing toys and books etc.

The people we are helping learn to appreciate our efforts – Life for them will improve in a positive way. There are so many ways to be generous with your gifts.

Are you prepared to be more generous in different ways?

Generosity Quotes

"We make a living by what we get, but we make a life by what we give."

Winston Churchill 1874-1965; British Orator, Author and Prime Minister during World War II.

"What we do for ourselves dies with us. What we do for others and the world remains and is immortal." Albert Pine, English Author, died 1851.

"He who cannot give anything away cannot feel anything either."

Fredrich Nietzsche 1844-1900, German classical scholar and Philosopher.

SUMMARY

Character Values are the common link

amongst all people of different cultures and faiths

In this current world of diverse nationalities all intermingled together, sharing character values can bring us together, emphasising the factors that bring unity, rather than quoting all our differences. Unity within our diverse society is essential to enhance peace and prosperity.

No one is perfect, we can only strive to improve ourselves and society we live in.

We believe that every human being has a well of character values within themselves, but time and life problems tend to make us suppress or hide these values as other things seem more important.

As a society we humans need positive feelings to connect the world:-

Positive Feelings = LOVE Negative Feelings = HATE Get rid of /or reduce negative feelings and the world **WILL** improve.

If people learn to APPRECIATE their blessings, they might learn to CARE for what they have, and therefore know how to RESPECT their own and other people's property, take RESPONSIBILITY for their own actions and gain some SELF-CONTROL.

Do you think that character values can reach and change people's attitudes, including those who are not spiritually minded or only think of today?

You may like to consider that that the three values, 'Appreciation', 'Caring' and 'Forgiveness', can make a huge difference to people's lives and can lead to using the remaining character values more effectively.

*"Fame is a vapour, popularity an accident, riches take wing and only character endures. "*Horace Greenley, 1811-1859; American journalist and educator.

"The measure of a man's character is what he would do if he knew he would never be found out." Baron Thomas Babington Macauley, 1800-1859; English Historian and Statesman.

It is hoped that the ten character values discussed in this book will be a drop in the ocean of humanity that will spread its ripples far and wide.

Printed in Great Britain
by Amazon

45749590R00066